HOT TOPICS

VIOLENT CRIME

Allison Lassieur

Heinemann LIBRARY

Chicago, Illinois

www.heinemannraintree.com
Visit our website to find out more information about Heinemann-Raintree books.

To order:
☎ Phone 888-454-2279
🖳 Visit www.heinemannraintree.com to browse our catalog and order online.

Edited by Adam Miller, Andrew Farrow, and Adrian Vigliano
Designed by Clare Webber and Steven Mead
Original illustrations © Capstone Global Library Ltd.
Picture research by Ruth Blair
Production by Eirian Griffiths
Originated by Capstone Global Library Ltd.
Printed and bound in China by Leo Paper Products Ltd.

15 14 13 12 11
10 9 8 7 6 5 4 3 2 1

Library of Congress Cataloging-in-Publication Data
Lassieur, Allison.
    Violent crime / Allison Louise Lassieur.
        p. cm.—(Hot topics)
    Includes bibliographical references and index.
    ISBN 978-1-4329-4874-0 (hc)
    1. Violent crimes—Juvenile literature.
    2. Violent crimes—Prevention—Juvenile literature. I. Title.
    HV6251.L37 2012
    364.15—dc22   2010046908

Acknowledgments
The author and publishers are grateful to the following for permission to reproduce copyright material: Corbis pp. **6** (© HO/Reuters), **10** (© Jon Naso/Star Ledger), **11** (© Steve Klaver/Star Ledger), **9** (© Andrew Aitchison/In Pictures), **14** (©Tony Savino), **21** (© Reuters), **25** (© LUKE MACGREGOR/Reuters), **33** (© Jairo Cajina/XinHua/Xinhua Press), **37** (© DANIEL AGUILAR/Reuters), **39** (EPA/ALEX CRUZ), **40** (© Antonio Lacerda/epa), **47** (© GLEB GARANICH/Reuters), **50** (© Roy McMahon); Getty Images pp. **12** (Robert Nickelserg), **26** (Bruno Vincent), **31** (Christopher Furlong), **44** (Michele Falzone), **49** (Bruno Vincent), **51** (Christopher Furlong); PA Photos p. **18** (Dave Caulkin/AP); Photolibrary pp. **5** (Splashdown Direct/OSF), **41** (EPA/STR); Shutterstock pp. **17** (© Tony Magdaraog), **29** (© corepics), **43** (© Jorge Pedro Barradas de Casais).

Cover photograph of a police officer arresting a man reproduced with permission of Corbis (© moodboard).

Every effort has been made to contact copyright holders of any material reproduced in this book. Any omissions will be rectified in subsequent printings if notice is given to the publisher.

CONTENTS

Some words are printed in bold, **like this**. You can find out what they mean by looking in the glossary.

A VIOLENT WORLD?

When you log onto the Internet or turn on the television, the headlines scream about violent crime. Depending on where you live, the stories might tell of gang shootings, knife fights, drug-related violence, or armed robbery. You can't escape it—it feels like violent crime is everywhere.

How does violent crime affect you?

While the media are full of these stories, for most people violent crime is not a part of day-to-day life. Very few people are unfortunate enough to be a victim—or a witness—to violence. But violent crime can touch almost everyone.

Even if you have never experienced violent crime, violent crime can still affect your way of life. If you don't think that is true, then ask yourself: Are there bars on the windows of your school? Are the teller windows at your local bank covered with thick Plexiglas? Do you have to go through a scanner when you enter a government building? These security measures are so commonplace that they are invisible to most people, but they are all there because of the threat of violent crime.

GOOD NEWS?

There is some good news out there. Statistically, the rate of violent crime around the world (with the exception of terrorism) is falling. It may not seem like it, but the world is a safer place now than it was when you were born. In the United States, for instance, violent crime has been on the decline since the 1990s. However, "lower" crime does not mean "no" crime—and so people and communities still struggle with violent crime every day.

There are many kinds of violent crime, ranging from robbery, to rape, to assault. This book's main focus will be gun, knife, and drug-related violence. We will examine different examples of these kinds of violence around the world, exploring how these kinds of crime affect people, what causes them in the first place, and what people can do to stop the cycle of violent crime.

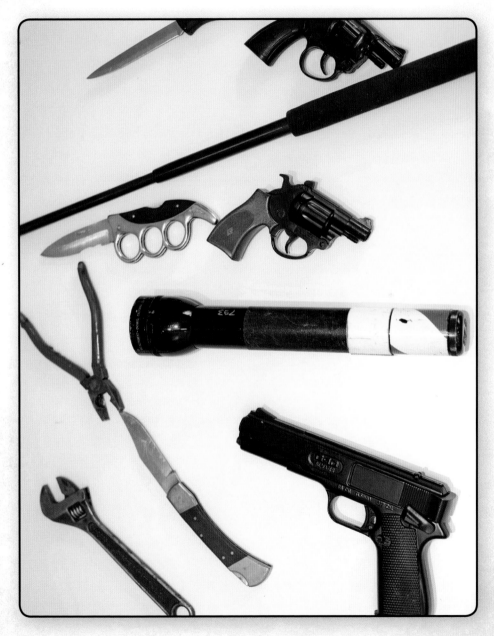

■ Even ordinary household tools like pliers and wrenches can be deadly weapons. These items were seized by police in Cumbria, UK.

GUN VIOLENCE IN SCHOOLS

Two school shootings

It was an ordinary school day at Jokela High School in Tuusula, Finland, on November 7, 2007. A few minutes before noon, students heard gunfire echoing through the halls. Eighteen-year-old Pekka-Eric Auvinen, a student, strode through the school firing a **semi-automatic** pistol at everyone he saw. By the time he was finished, 6 students, the school nurse, and the principal were dead, and 12 people were wounded. Police found Auvinen in a bathroom with a gunshot wound to the head.

■ Pekka-Eric Auvinen posted a YouTube video predicting the massacre just a few hours before he opened fire.

Less than a year later, and halfway around the world, school was just about to start at Central High School in Knoxville, Tennessee, on Thursday, August 21, 2008. Students were gathered in the cafeteria when two students, Ryan McDonald and Jamar Siler, began arguing. Suddenly McDonald staggered away, clutching his chest and bleeding. Siler walked away.

Most people in the crowded cafeteria had not heard the gunshot over the noise in the room. Doctors pronounced McDonald dead less than an hour later. Siler was arrested and charged with murder. They were both 15 years old.

Why did they do it?

At first glance, these two shootings, which happened worlds away from one another, seem to have little in common. Auvinen was a decent student with a stable home life. Siler was a loner with a minor criminal record and a troubled family.

Statistics show that people who face violence and instability in their personal lives are more likely to turn to violence than those who do not. This is one theory why people turn to guns and violence, and it helps explain cases like that of Jamar Siler. But not everyone who picks up a gun comes from a bad home—this is shown by the case of Pekka-Eric Auvinen.

Bullying

The boys in both cases did have one thing in common: they had both been victims of bullies at school. Some people have more trouble handling unusual stresses like being bullied than others do. People who feel powerless or out of control might pick up a gun because it makes them feel in control and strong, or because they think it will help them gain respect.

Often it is a combination of several of these factors—both at home and at school—that leads to gun violence in schools. But it is hard to know, or to predict, exactly why gun violence happens in schools. It is this unpredictability that makes it so frightening.

A SAFE PLACE TO BE?

While stories of school shootings can cause fear, it is important to remember that, overall, schools are a safe place for people to be. In the United States, less than 1 percent of all youths killed by guns since 1992 have been in school. That does not mean that schools can ignore safety issues. But, at the same time, students should not live in fear.

Zero-tolerance policies

In response to these sorts of tragedies, governments and schools are searching for solutions. One idea is "**zero-tolerance**" policies, which many schools in the United States and Europe have implemented over the last few years.

These policies started appearing in U.S. schools in the mid-1990s, during the height of a "get tough on crime" attitude throughout society. In 1994 the U.S. government passed a law that required states getting federal money to suspend—for a year—any student caught with a weapon at school. The goal was to make school safer for everyone.

Flawed results

On the surface, a zero-tolerance policy sounds like a good, easy way to get rid of problem students. But, in reality, these policies have not reduced violent crime. They have also caused new problems.

One of the biggest failures of zero-tolerance policies is that they do not leave any room for judgment or common sense. There are dozens of stories of kids who have accidentally, or unknowingly, brought bread knives, plastic knives, or water pistols to school, only to be suspended or expelled as a result. For example, in February 2010, nine-year-old Patrick Timoney was nearly suspended for taking a 5-centimeter (2-inch) plastic LEGO toy to school.

Zero tolerance has failed in other ways, too. Students removed from school, with nothing to do, tend to drop out more frequently and get into more trouble with the law. There is also no evidence that the zero-tolerance policy has kept weapons out of schools any more than other policies do.

Most people argue that, if zero-tolerance policies are going to work, teachers and administrators must be allowed to use their judgment and common sense when determining whether something is a threat, rather than being forced to follow a rigid zero-tolerance policy.

THE SCHOOL-TO-JAIL PIPELINE

Zero-tolerance policies have created something called a school-to-jail pipeline. Honest kids who have made one mistake, like forgetting a plastic water gun in their backpack, suddenly find themselves with suspension on their school record—and, in extreme cases, a police record—instead of going to the principal's office. How do you think this would feel? What kind of long-term effects would this have?

■ A guard escorts a young inmate through a juvenile detention facility. Critics of zero-tolerance policies have argued that these policies create circumstances that may push students down a path that leads to situations like detention, rather than helping students avoid these problems.

School security

Another approach to school gun violence is increased security. More and more, especially in the United States, schools are installing prison-like security throughout their buildings. Bars, fences, metal detectors, video **surveillance**, and even armed security guards are becoming common sights.

■ Some schools employ security teams to monitor students throughout the day. It's routine for security to search students every time they leave the building.

The idea for prison-like school security was unheard of until the 1990s, when school shootings were on the rise around the United States. In recent years other countries, such as the United Kingdom and Finland, have considered measures to increase school security in the wake of shootings in their own schools.

Sometimes, though, tough security does more harm than good. Studies have shown that schools with lots of security make students and faculty feel anxious and fearful rather than safe. The security makes them feel more like criminals than students and teachers.

TEACHERS WITH GUNS?

One solution that has been proposed to stop violent gun crimes is to allow teachers to bring their own guns to school. The idea is that if teachers are armed, students are less likely to bring, or use, weapons in school. How would you feel if you knew your teachers were carrying weapons in class? Would it make school feel safer?

A targeted approach

Some people argue that a more effective security strategy is to focus on likely sources of violence, rather than an entire school. Only a small percentage of all students in the United States tend to commit criminal acts. But this small group is responsible for a large percentage of all crimes in schools. If a school can identify these problem students, this is a first step to safety.

It also helps to identify the kinds of crimes these dangerous students commit. That way, a school can put security in place that will eliminate that specific type of crime. For example, the best security at a school facing weapon violence might be metal detectors, but a school grappling with drug violence might need locker checks and drug-sniffing dogs instead.

■ Security cameras have become commonplace in many U.S. schools. This camera watches students in the cafeteria at a New Jersey school.

Stopping trouble before it starts

Recently, more schools around the world have started taking a different approach. They are working harder to help the students whom they identify as likely to cause trouble. By talking to therapists or peer groups, it is hoped that these kids will work through their anger or aggression before they express it through violence.

Anti-bullying programs, after-school activities, peer support groups, and a focus on conflict resolution are some things schools in Europe and Canada, as well as the United States, are also trying to get kids back on the right path.

GUNS AND GANG VIOLENCE

When people think of gun violence, they often think of gangs. In recent years, the problem of guns and gang violence has been spreading throughout the world, from the United States to Europe, from China to the Caribbean—in both large cities and small towns. (See pages 22 to 23 for hotspots around the world.)

Numbers and firepower

How do gangs gain their power? It is partly because of sheer numbers. For instance, in 2008 there were about one million gang members in the United States, and only about 700,000 police officers. That is more than one gang member for every officer in the whole country.

■ Los Angeles police are seen here arresting several gang members in Los Angeles. The suspects were part of a local tagging gang—a group that paints gang graffiti. Large organized street gangs recruit from these smaller youth gangs.

Organized street gangs also gain power because they are some of the best-armed groups in the world. In the United States, local police districts do not have the money to buy the same high-end assault weapons that the gangs can get. Moreover, many state or local laws prohibit (prevent) police from carrying certain types of weapons—which often ensures that police will be outgunned in a firefight with gang members.

Percent of homicides involving guns by circumstances, 1976-2005

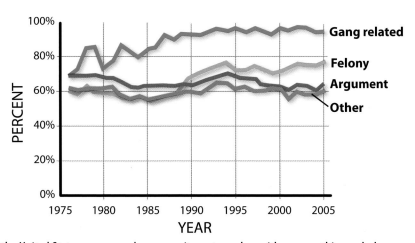

■ In the United States, gang members commit most murders with guns, as this graph shows.

Many countries ban guns, which means that guns are harder for gangs to get—but gangs still manage to get guns. In some countries, such as the United Kingdom, Norway, and New Zealand, most police officers are unarmed. This puts them at a great disadvantage when dealing with well-armed gangs, and it makes for potentially dangerous situations.

ARMING LONDON POLICE OFFICERS

In response to the rise of gun violence, in 2009 some London police officers began carrying semi-automatic weapons while on duty in certain areas of the city. It was the first time in UK history that police officers were armed while on regular patrol.

CASE STUDY

Newburgh, New York: When gangs overrun a town

In downtown Newburgh, New York, boarded-up storefronts are covered in graffiti. Residents hesitate to go out at night. Located an hour north of New York City, the run-down town has been torn apart by gangs and guns.

Even though Newburgh is a small city, with only 29,000 residents, it has the highest rate of crime **per capita** in the whole state of New York. The city is overrun with both national gangs, like the Latin Kings and the Bloods, and homegrown gangs like D-Block and Ashley Bandits. The police are overwhelmed—some estimates suggest gang members outnumber police officers three to one. With those odds, the gangs have become fearless.

Police are fighting back, though, and are teaming with the Federal Bureau of Investigation (FBI) to end the violence. On May 13, 2010, a huge raid by FBI and local police resulted in the arrests of about two-dozen gang members. Police already had 34 gang members in prison, so arresting the others made the raid a huge success for law enforcement. The reality, though, is that the gangs were damaged, but not destroyed. It will take a lot more effort, money, and firepower for police to clean up Newburgh.

■ New York police can be seen here arresting a group of gang members in Newburgh.

Where do gangs get their firepower?

How do gangs get their huge supplies of weapons? They usually get guns illegally, buying them on the street. These weapons were usually stolen or illegally purchased in the first place, or sometimes bought online. The privacy of online purchases makes the Internet a good source for illegal guns and other weapons. Guns used by gangs change hands a lot, so they are tough for police to track if they are used in a violent crime.

Many of the big international gangs have the numbers—and the power—to get illegally imported weapons. Because the United States has looser gun restrictions than many other countries (see page 17), many gangs from other countries get their guns from there.

For example, the powerful Mexican drug **cartels** (see pages 36 to 39) buy guns by the thousands from U.S. dealers. In fact, 90 percent of all the illegal weapons used by Mexican drug gangs come from the United States. Many powerful gangs in Europe also illegally **smuggle** guns in from the United States or from Eastern Europe.

CASE STUDY

Guns in the Caribbean

The U.S. Virgin Islands, Jamaica, and Trinidad and Tobago have recently developed powerful gangs that are central to international drug trafficking. These gangs are very well armed, often with weapons from the United States. Jamaican officials, for example, report that 80 percent of the weapons they confiscate can be traced back to the United States.

Gang violence in the Caribbean is spilling over into the high schools there as well, where teen gangs are getting stronger—and getting their own guns. Almost half of high school students there report having seen a weapon at school, and 25 percent of all kids are part of a gang. Gun violence in the Caribbean is so new that law enforcement has not had time to get it under control.

THE GUN CONTROL DEBATE

Given all the headlines about school shootings, gang slayings, and other violent gun crimes, something needs to be done. But what is the best way to move forward?

Differing opinions

The question of gun control ignites heated debate. Some people believe that guns lead to violence—and that it is obvious that guns should be banned altogether. Other people, however, think that guns play an important role in sporting and hunting (see box below) and should be allowed in certain circumstances. Still other people, especially in the United States, argue that the right to bear arms—meaning the right to carry a gun—is an essential freedom that should not be regulated by the government (see page 20).

GUNS AND HUNTING

In some parts of the world, hunting is a normal part of local life. Generations have hunted for deer, bear, and other animals, and the tradition is passed down. Supporters of hunting argue that it plays a crucial role in keeping local populations of animals from getting too high. Moreover, the economies of regions with good hunting grounds rely on hunting season, as visiting hunters pay for lodging, food, supplies, and more. For example, in 2006 alone, deer hunting brought $500 million to the state of Michigan's economy.

Laws

People with these varying opinions will never agree completely, but there are ways to use laws to make gun ownership safer for everyone. Most countries around the world have gun laws that are strictly enforced. In the United Kingdom, Spain, Italy, Germany, France, and the Netherlands, for instance, all gun owners must have a license, and in many cases only hunters or sportspeople are allowed to get a license. Most countries require firearms to be registered. Countries with these kinds of laws tend to have lower violent gun crime rates than the rest of the world.

Most countries also have penalties for the possession or sale of illegal guns. Gun owners like these laws because they punish criminals who use guns, but without restricting the legal right to own guns. These laws do put more criminals behind bars for longer sentences, but they do not keep guns off the streets altogether.

■ Soldiers at a parade booth in Manila, Philippines. Recent estimates show that the Philippines have the most gun-related deaths in Asia, which has sparked a debate over the country's relatively loose gun control laws.

CASE STUDY

Strict gun control in the United Kingdom

At one end of the spectrum of gun control is the United Kingdom. It has the most restrictive gun laws in the world, guaranteeing that few people can legally own a firearm.

But this was not always the case. Until the late 1980s, attitudes toward gun ownership in the UK were fairly relaxed. Then two grisly mass murders occurred that completely changed the country's attitude toward guns. Because of these killings, the UK government passed a series of gun laws that all but banned most guns from the country.

The Hungerford massacre

At first no one paid attention to the 27-year-old, scruffy man in combat-style camouflage clothing roaming the quiet town of Hungerford, England. Then, shots began to ring through the streets. The semi-automatic rifle Michael Ryan was using was so accurate that it could hit a target at 300 meters (328 yards), and he was pointing and shooting at anyone he happened to see.

Among his victims were a police officer, and a woman on a picnic with her children. Later, his mother was found dead, probably his first victim. By the time police cornered the shooter in a local school, he had killed 16 people and wounded 15 others. Before the police could arrest him, he killed himself. Later, he would be described as a loner and a gun fanatic.

■ Blankets cover a taxi in Hungerford, England. Inside is the body of one of the victims of gunman Michael Ryan.

In response to this tragedy, the UK government passed an **amendment** to the Firearms Act law, banning ownership of semi-automatic and pump-action rifles, weapons that fire explosive **ammunition**, short shotguns with **magazines** and elevated **pump action**, and self-loading rifles.

The Dunblane massacre

On March 13, 1996, 43-year-old Thomas Hamilton, a former Scout leader, walked into a school in Dunblane, Scotland, and headed for the gym, where a group of five- and six-year-olds were having gym class. There, he pulled out a handgun and started spraying bullets at the children. Then, he walked down the hall and attacked another classroom, before returning to the gym and killing himself. Hamilton killed 16 children and their teacher, and he wounded 12 other children. At the time of the shooting, Hamilton owned six legal handguns and had licenses for them.

In 1997, in response to this massacre—the worst mass murder in UK history—the UK government passed a law totally banning handguns, including pistols and .22-caliber guns.

THE CUMBRIA SHOOTINGS—WILL THEY LEAD TO MORE RESTRICTIONS?

More recently, UK residents were shaken on June 2, 2010, with the horrible news of a grisly massacre in Cumbria, in northwest England. A 52-year-old cab driver named Derrick Bird killed 12 people and wounded 11 others.

Some organizations are calling for even stricter gun control laws in the aftermath of the mass murder. But Prime Minister David Cameron cautioned "not to leap to knee-jerk conclusions" about the need for tougher laws.

What do you think? How should governments react to violent gun crimes like the Cumbria massacre? Are new, stricter laws the answer?

Loose gun laws in the United States

The United States represents the opposite extreme on the spectrum of gun control, with some of the loosest gun laws in the world.

In the United States, if people want to get a gun legally, they follow a basic set of rules, such as background checks. But there are ways around these laws. To begin with, each state is allowed to make laws regulating the sale, ownership, and use of guns. As a result, people can buy a gun from a state with much looser requirements than their own state.

Popular events known as gun shows are another easy way for people to get guns. At these gatherings, licensed gun-show sellers are required to follow a state's gun regulations. But in many states, unlicensed sellers and private citizens can sell at gun shows, too—and they do not have to follow the law. These sellers provide assault weapons, handguns, shotguns, rifles, and even military weapons. When they sell a weapon, there is no paperwork and no background check—just an exchange of cash.

Disagreement

Many people in the United States have called for changes to many of these laws. However, the issue of gun control is heatedly debated in the United States because the "right to bear arms" is a part of U.S. history and the U.S. Constitution (see box below). U.S. citizens and the U.S. government debate gun control measures whenever a new gun-related tragedy happens, just as in other countries. But it is difficult to reach consensus on this topic in the United States.

THE SECOND AMENDMENT

The Second Amendment to the U.S. Constitution reads: "A well regulated militia being necessary to the security of a free State, the right of the People to keep and bear arms shall not be infringed." For supporters of gun rights, this means gun ownership is an individual right that should not be tampered with. Supporters of gun control argue, however, that the wording suggests members of the military have a right to be armed— but everyday citizens do not. Debate over the interpretation of this amendment—and how this 1791 amendment can be applied to today's realities of gun violence—continue to rage on.

Crimes committed with firearms, 1973-2006

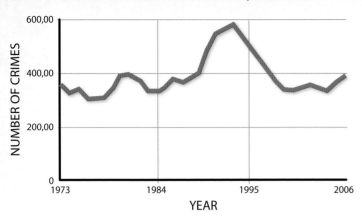

■ This graph traces violent gun crime in the U.S. over about three decades. The spiking violence seen in the late 1980s through the early 1990s is often linked to the rise in crack cocaine use in that period of time.

CASE STUDY

The Columbine massacre and gun shows

In April 1999, near Littleton, Colorado, Eric Harris and Dylan Klebold went on a shooting rampage at their high school, killing 13 people and wounding over 20 more. They had acquired some of their guns at a gun show. They had first tried to buy the guns themselves, but they were denied because both boys were under 18. Several gun retailers at the show told them to return with a friend who was 18, so they did. Their friend, Robyn Anderson, was happy to help. She only went to private sellers.

All she had to do was show proof that she was 18, and she bought all the guns Eric and Dylan picked out. No one questioned them.

■ A security camera at Columbine High School captured this image of Dylan Klebold and Eric Harris.

Gun violence rate and gun ownership rates—a connection?

The countries listed on this map have the most civilian gun ownership in the world—but not always the most gun violence. These numbers prove that unraveling the causes of gun violence are not always as straightforward as keeping guns away from people.

United States
In the United States, 88 out of every 100 people own a firearm. Ownership laws vary from state to state, but most people can legally purchase a gun. In 2006, 68 percent of all murders were committed with guns.

Finland

In Finland, 45 out of every 100 people own a firearm. Anyone 15 years old or older can apply for a gun license, and most gun owners are hunters or members of shooting and hunting clubs. Gun violence is rare, possibly because most weapons are hunting guns, not small arms such as handguns.

Switzerland

In Switzerland, 46 out of every 100 people own a firearm. All male Swiss citizens are required to serve in the military and are issued with firearms, which they keep. Laws restrict civilian gun ownership. Swiss citizens respect gun ownership as part of a patriotic military service. Gun violence rates are so low that records are not kept.

Yemen

In Yemen, 55 out of every 100 people own a firearm. There are no laws restricting gun ownership. Gun violence is soaring in Yemen, with more than 35,000 gun-related crimes committed in 2005.

Serbia

In Serbia, 37 out of every 100 people own a firearm. The Serbia–Kosovo conflict in the 1990s left Serbia awash with firearms, and today there are more than three million guns owned by civilians. But gun violence is very low. In 2006 guns killed only 47 people.

KNIFE VIOLENCE

As we have seen, some countries have passed laws that severely limit the number of guns that get into people's hands. But this does not mean that violent crime does not happen in other ways. In many countries—ranging from the United Kingdom to Australia to South Africa to China—knife crime is increasingly becoming a serious problem.

What, exactly, is knife crime? It is any violent, criminal act committed with a bladed weapon, which includes everything from small penknives to samurai swords.

KNIFE CRIME IN THE UNITED KINGDOM

Knife crime has become an especially hot topic in the United Kingdom. Even though the overall crime rate in the UK has steadily fallen since the 1990s, the rate of knife crimes has risen—and the biggest jump has happened since 2005. Between 2005 and 2007, knife **homicides** rose 26 percent. This was the greatest increase of any kind of violent crime in the UK to date.

Knife Injuries as proportion of all serious injuries 1994-2008

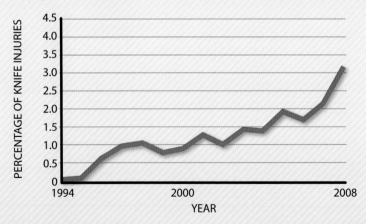

■ One way to track the rise of knife violence is to study how many people report injuries caused by knives.

Young people and knives

What makes recent trends in knife violence particularly alarming is that many of the people responsible for knife crimes are kids or teens. A typical knife owner is usually a male around 19 years old, but could be a kid as young as 6 or 7. He lives in a rough part of a big city and runs with a group of friends. Kids of all races and ethnicities carry knives. The thing they often have in common is poverty. Across the board, they tend to be poor, without a lot of options for improvement.

The biggest question is, why knives? The answer is easy: because they are cheap and easy for young people to get their hands on. Anyone can grab a kitchen knife out of the house, for instance. Any blade 7.5 centimeters (3 inches) or shorter, such as penknives, are legal, so lots of kids carry them. Switchblades are popular, even though they are illegal, and they are not hard to get on the street or online.

■ From kitchen knives to box cutters, almost any kind of knife can be used in violent crimes. These blades were seized by UK police from various operations around the country.

Knife crime and gangs

In many places, the recent rise in knife crimes is believed to be connected to rises in gangs. The areas most affected by knife violence are often in poor, **urban** areas—the kinds of places where gangs are most prevalent. This was the case in the sad story of Kodjo Yenga (see below).

CASE STUDY

Kodjo Yenga

At age 16, Kodjo Yenga was a star student, well liked by family and friends. His dream was to go to college, which he was on track to do. He was a confident, strong young man who became another grim statistic of knife violence on March 14, 2007.

Kodjo and his girlfriend were out that evening in London when he was approached by a 15-year-old who said, "I hear you want to fight me." Kodjo then did something no one should do when faced with a threat: Kodjo took the boy up on the threat and followed him to a side street. To Kodjo's surprise, a mob of teenagers armed with knives and bats was waiting.

■ Mourners hold up a photo of Kodjo Yenga as they march through the streets of London after his death in 2007. He was one of 26 London teenagers to die as a result of knife violence that year.

The gang chased after Kodjo, shouting, "Catch him" and "Kill him." The gang caught Kodjo and he went down. His girlfriend and passers-by tried to save him, but he died not long after the attack.

It wasn't long before police arrested several members of the gang. Their gang, MDP, had a reputation for violence and carrying knives. Most of the gang members were under 18 years old. The problems had started a few months before, when Kodjo had a run-in with some MDP members at a club. From then on he was a target, until the gang finally caught him.

In April 2008 five teens were found guilty in the attack. One killer was 17 years old, and the other only 14. They were sentenced to life in prison. The other three—14, 15, and 17 years old, respectively—were each given 10-year sentences.

Percentages of UK crimes in which a knife was used, 1995-2008

Year	Wounding		Robbery		Common assault		All violence	
	Estimate number	% of all incidents	Estimate number	% of all incidents	Estimate number	% of all incidents	Estimate number	% of all incidents
1995	84,000	9	97,000	23	160,000	5	334,000	8
1997	37,000	5	55,000	17	77,000	3	180,000	5
1999	61,000	9	72,000	18	53,000	2	194,000	5
2001/2	64,000	10	63,000	18	63,000	4	191,000	7
2002/3	41,000	6	58,000	19	128,000	8	217,000	8
2003/4	29,000	4	30,000	10	70,000	4	125,000	5
2004/5	29,000	5	26,000	10	89,000	6	139,000	6
2005/6	34,000	6	41,000	18	90,000	6	157,000	7
2006/7	38,000	7	65,000	20	140,000	9	181,000	7
2007/8	38,000	8	48,000	15	53,000	4	138,000	6

Knife crimes in Australian schools

A particularly troubling recent development has been knife crimes in schools. In recent years a series of knife crimes in Australian schools have shocked the nation. While most incidents involved students threatening other students with knives, on February 15, 2010, something far more tragic happened. In Brisbane, a 12-year-old boy named Elliott Fletcher was stabbed to death in a bathroom at a Catholic boys' school. His attacker was another student who was just 13 years old.

In the days after the killing, parents and the media tried to make sense of the tragedy. Reports said that the attacker was a good student who did not cause any problems, but that the bullying culture at school had made him feel he needed a knife for protection. As the story became discussed more widely, Australian officials became aware of more and more reports that a culture of knife violence was becoming common in many Australian schools, with students bringing knives to gain a sense of power—or protection.

Knife crimes in Chinese schools

In the spring of 2010, China was shocked by a series of nine deadly knife attacks in schools. At least 17 people were killed and dozens more were injured as a result of these attacks.

Unlike the attacks in Australia, however, in China the attackers were all grown men. In one attack, a 42-year-old doctor stabbed 8 students to death and wounded 5 others as the children waited outside their school. In another attack, a man entered a kindergarten and stabbed 31 people, including 28 students.

How could this have happened?

The world watched in horror as these attacks occurred. What would cause these men to do such a thing? While there are no simple answers, a common theme was that many of the attackers suffered from mental illness that had not been properly treated.

In most cases, the attackers were angry at the world and wanted to send a "message" about how they felt they had been wronged. In China, there was almost no security to protect children in schools, and so, sadly, schools became an easy, shocking target where the men could do the most possible damage and gain media attention.

KNIVES INSTEAD OF GUNS?

In Australia only about 5 percent of adults own guns. In China the government prevents its citizens from owning guns at all. Given these statistics, it makes sense that violent criminals in these countries end up using what is available to them—knives.

People who support gun ownership rights often point to these sorts of stories of knife violence. They argue that these stories prove that if people are going to be violent, they will find a way to do it—with or without guns. They believe this proves that banning guns is not the answer. What do you think?

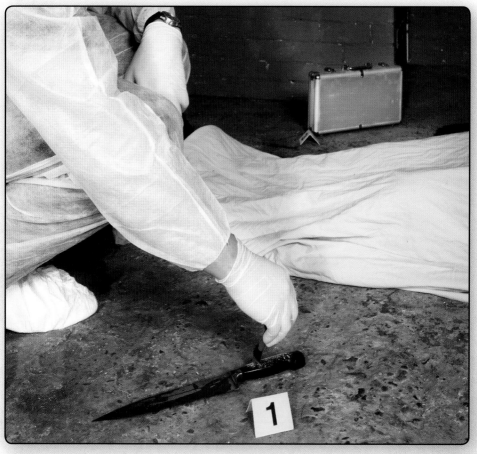

■ Many governments and law enforcement agencies around the world are trying to find new ways to reduce knife crime.

Solutions to knife crime

Given all these tragedies, something clearly needs to be done about knife crime. One obvious problem in restricting many kinds of knives is that, unlike guns, knives have a place in everyday life—for example, in kitchens—and cannot be banned or restricted in the same way guns can.

Some people argue that police should have the right to search suspects—often young people—if they think these people might pose a threat of knife violence. In the United Kingdom, however, where "**stop and search**" laws have been introduced, this issue is deeply controversial (see box at right).

Other people think that there needs to be more awareness about the issue of knife violence. The countries most touched by the problem, such as the United Kingdom, have started major advertising campaigns against knife violence, using television, radio, and even Facebook.

In Australia, politicians are discussing similar advertising campaigns. In response to recent knife violence in schools, new attention has also been given to anti-bullying programs in schools there.

Safety in schools

In Australia, again in response to recent school violence, some parents have asked for increased security measures at school. But Deputy Prime Minister Julia Gillard supported a measured response, saying, "So we don't want to just, you know, wake up and be in America with metal detectors and security guards with guns standing outside school gates. I think we've got to work through school by [school] . . . and work with them to get the right response."

During the knife attacks in China, the Chinese Ministry of Education began to create stricter safety standards for its schools, including registering visitors, having more security guards on site, and installing security systems. The government is also considering ways to teach kids to protect themselves.

STOP AND SEARCH

Two UK laws give police the power to search anyone, at any point, without suspicion of a crime. In the mid-1990s the first such law, known as Section 60, was created to deal with things like fights after sporting events and gang violence. Later, Section 44 was created to catch terrorists by giving police power to stop anyone in designated areas.

In 2008 UK police got the idea to use Section 60 to combat knife violence everywhere. Since then the number of Section 60 "stop and searches" has exploded in London and other large cities. In London alone, stop and searches went from about 4,400 in 2003–2004 to more than 80,000 in 2008–2009.

According to official reports, stop and search has taken thousands of knives off the streets, and law enforcement officials insist that these laws have reduced some knife crime. But other studies suggest that in some areas, knife crime has increased since police began using Section 60.

A growing number of people find stop and search very intrusive and against the spirit of UK law. Police stop and search teens far more often than adults. There is also some compelling evidence to suggest that minorities are searched more often than whites. Recently the UK government revoked Section 44. A growing number of people hope the government gets rid of Section 60 next.

■ Police stop and search a group of partygoers arriving in Liverpool, England, who have come to the city to celebrate the Christmas holiday.

DRUGS AND VIOLENT CRIME

In July 2010, an alarming travel warning was released by the U.S. State Department about a small Mexican town called Nuevo Laredo, on the border between Mexico and the United States. The warning said: "We have received credible reports of widespread violence occurring now, between **narcotics** trafficking organizations and the Mexican Army in Nuevo Laredo. We have credible reports of **grenades** being used. The narcotics traffickers have reportedly blocked at least one major avenue, Lopez de Lara, and are **carjacking** vehicles. Other roads may also be blocked by narcotics traffickers."

As this example shows, Mexico is being torn apart by drug violence. In response, since 2008 the Mexican and U.S. governments have engaged in a joint effort to bring down powerful Mexican drug cartels. Some estimates say more than 7,000 people have died in only about a year—many of them Americans—and the violence continues.

FIREPOWER

Where did Mexican drug cartels get such amazing firepower, including grenades? Ironically, many of the grenades that the Mexican drug cartels are throwing at U.S. and Mexican forces were made in the United States. They are part of **ammunition** that was sold to Central American countries decades ago to aid them in civil wars during the 1980s. Now some of those countries are dusting off their weapon stockpiles and selling them to the highest bidders: the drug lords of Mexico.

A global problem

But drug-related violence is not just a Mexican problem. Around the world, drugs fuel all kinds of violence, from shootouts in Afghanistan to stabbings in London and shootings in Jamaica. Central and South American countries such as Bolivia and Colombia have been experiencing terrible violence for years, fueled by powerful drug cartels that control the cocaine industry. In the Middle East, the Taliban, a powerful movement in Afghanistan, gets most of its estimated income of $70 million a year from opium. Opium is made from the poppy plants that grow in Afghanistan, and it is processed into heroin.

■ Police in Nicaragua are shown here arresting a leader of the international criminal gang MS-13. The MS-13 gang, which is notoriously violent and dangerous, has reportedly become involved with Mexican drug cartels and their drug trafficking activities.

Illegal drugs around the world

The worldwide trade in illegal drugs is often linked closely to violent crime. This map highlights some of the countries that are most affected by these problems.

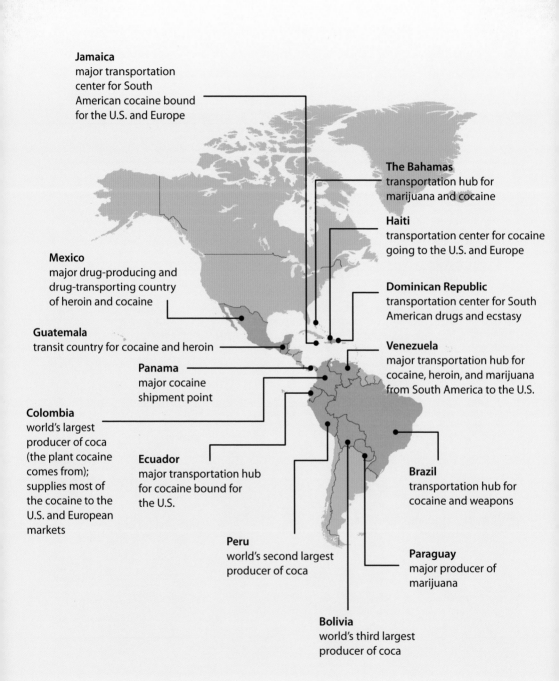

Jamaica
major transportation center for South American cocaine bound for the U.S. and Europe

The Bahamas
transportation hub for marijuana and cocaine

Haiti
transportation center for cocaine going to the U.S. and Europe

Mexico
major drug-producing and drug-transporting country of heroin and cocaine

Dominican Republic
transportation center for South American drugs and ecstasy

Guatemala
transit country for cocaine and heroin

Venezuela
major transportation hub for cocaine, heroin, and marijuana from South America to the U.S.

Panama
major cocaine shipment point

Colombia
world's largest producer of coca (the plant cocaine comes from); supplies most of the cocaine to the U.S. and European markets

Ecuador
major transportation hub for cocaine bound for the U.S.

Brazil
transportation hub for cocaine and weapons

Peru
world's second largest producer of coca

Paraguay
major producer of marijuana

Bolivia
world's third largest producer of coca

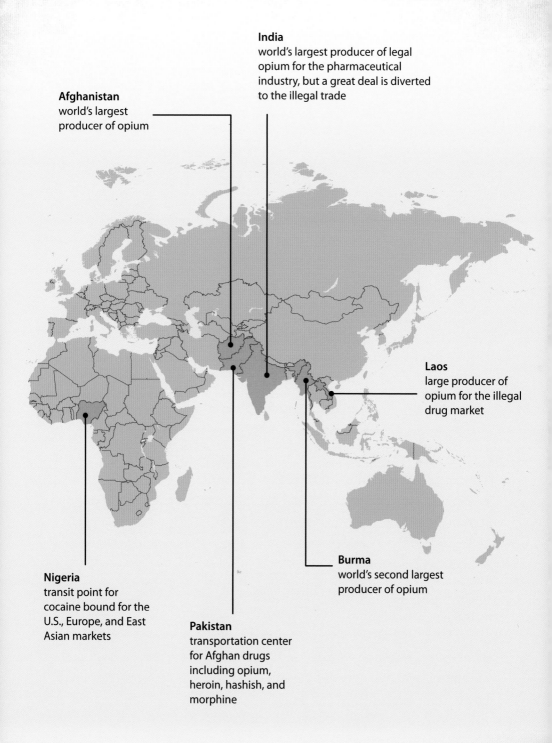

India
world's largest producer of legal opium for the pharmaceutical industry, but a great deal is diverted to the illegal trade

Afghanistan
world's largest producer of opium

Laos
large producer of opium for the illegal drug market

Nigeria
transit point for cocaine bound for the U.S., Europe, and East Asian markets

Burma
world's second largest producer of opium

Pakistan
transportation center for Afghan drugs including opium, heroin, hashish, and morphine

Created by violence

When people use drugs, their first thought is not where the drugs came from. But almost every type of drug that anyone uses today has been grown, made, moved, protected, or sold through some kind of violence.

Sometimes this violence is armed robbery, sometimes it is assault, and sometimes it is murder. Kidnapping is also recently on the rise. Most of the violent crimes drug cartels commit are against other local drug dealers or government officials who pose a threat to them. Sometimes attacks are for an unpaid debt. Other times the groups are stealing drugs from each other.

BIG MONEY

What is the motivation behind all of this drug-related violence? It is money, pure and simple. It is hard to know exactly how much money is involved, but some estimates suggest drug trafficking brings in more than $350 billion a year. In the United States alone, about $17.2 billion worth of illegal drugs—equal to the entire Canadian military budget— flows into the country from Mexico. When this much money is at stake, people get desperate—and violent.

The reach of Mexican cartels

The biggest, most dangerous, and most violent drug cartels in the world today are the Mexican cartels. (See pages 38 and 39 for a case study of La Familia, one of the most violent cartels.) These cartels extend their reach well beyond Mexico.

For instance, U.S. law enforcement has identified 230 U.S. cities—from Anchorage, Alaska, to Boston, Massachusetts, to Billings, Montana—where violent Mexican drug cartels have set up complex **distribution networks**, or where they supply drugs to local distributors. They create local **cells** of people who are willing to continue the cycle of violence and bring it to small towns and big cities across the United States.

In the last several years Mexican cartels have expanded, setting up shop in Europe and Central America, where they work with local crime organizations. In some of these countries, the Mexican cartels operate openly, especially in areas where the governments are weak or unstable. In Guatemala, Honduras, and El Salvador, the murder rates due to drug violence are even higher than in Mexico and the United States. The cartels use Venezuela as one of their busiest drug-trafficking hubs. Between 2006 and 2008, over half of all the cocaine in Europe came from Venezuela.

Violence has also skyrocketed in West Africa in the last few years, as the Mexican cartels, along with other Latin American drug organizations, joined forces with local gangs and crime families to distribute cocaine and other drugs around the world.

■ A guard, masked for his own safety, stands over cocaine seized in a 2007 operation. This shipment was hidden between the floor coverings of a Hong Kong container ship on its way to Mexico.

CASE STUDY

La Familia

Even by the standards of Mexican drug cartels, La Familia stands out as the most violent organization to rise in recent years. The group's taste for brutality was clearly shown in 2006, when Familia members rolled five severed heads onto a disco floor with a note saying, "This is divine justice." The group is known for killing its rivals with ice picks and boiling them to death, then severing heads and limbs before finally dumping the bodies.

The group, led by Nazario Gonzalez, known as El Mas Loco ("The Craziest One"), started out as a **vigilante** group that was supposed to act as a "good guy" by destroying drug dealers. Soon the group figured out that the drug business was a well-paying one, and in 2006 it broke away from the larger Gulf cartel group and rose fast. Today, La Familia is the largest supplier of meth to the United States, owning large "super labs" that produce hundreds of tons of meth a month.

All members of La Familia are required to carry a "bible" of divine sayings written by El Mas Loco, and all of their killings are considered "divine justice." Members are also prohibited from using drugs or alcohol, and they preach respect and honor toward women and children.

La Familia members believe it is their god-given right to destroy other cartels and take over their businesses, so that they can use the money to help poor families get food, shelter, and other necessities that government organizations cannot provide. This "steal from the rich, give to the poor" attitude makes local people loyal to the cartel—and reluctant to help law enforcement arrest them.

La Familia quickly spread to the United States and took control of the drug trade in several large U.S. cities. In October 2009, the U.S. and Mexican governments launched Project Coronado, arresting more than 300 members in 19 different U.S. states. It was the largest-ever raid against a Mexican drug cartel operating in the United States. In Colorado, for instance, authorities found cocaine, meth, and over $300,000. The raid was a huge success, but it only disrupted—and did not destroy—La Familia.

■ These alleged contract killers, working for the La Familia drug cartel, were arrested by Mexican authorities in 2010.

Young people, drugs, and violence

The headlines are filled with dramatic stories of drug cartel violence. Sometimes these stories involve young people (see box at right).

But, more commonly, young people who get caught up in drugs become involved in smaller-scale types of crime. The drugs of choice for most people under 21 who experiment are alcohol and marijuana. To get money for more alcohol or marijuana, kids may start stealing cash from family and friends, or taking things from home and selling them at school or on the street. They begin to get caught in a sad reality: people who use drugs are more likely to commit crimes.

Addictive drugs and violence

Most young people who use drugs do not move on to drugs like heroin or meth. But for drug users who do go on to try these "harder," highly addictive drugs, research shows that as the drugs become harder their crimes become more violent. Also, people who abuse lots of different drugs tend to commit some of the most violent crimes.

■ Brazilian police arrest a man during a 2007 raid. The drug bust involved almost 200 officers and shut down a cocaine lab able to produce up to 750 kilograms (1,650 pounds) of cocaine a month.

As people become addicted to drugs, they become increasingly willing to do whatever they need to do to support their addiction. That is when committing a violent crime, like armed robbery, starts to sound like a realistic possibility to an addict. In this way, the desperation of addicts creates even more drug-related violence.

CASE STUDY

Rosalio Reta: Teenage drug cartel assassin

"It was like being Superman or James Bond." Nineteen-year-old Rosalio Reta, an American, wasn't talking about a video game. He was talking about killing people—as a paid assassin for the powerful Mexican drug organization called the Gulf Cartel. For two years Reta and several other U.S. teenagers were paid to kill people for what was then the Gulf Cartel's assassin organization, Los Zetas. The boys had a nice house, nice cars, and were paid $500 a week to wait for orders. A successful kill could bring as much as $50,000 and two kilograms (4.4 pounds) of cocaine to the assassin. When Reta was arrested in 2006, he confessed to more than 30 killings.

■ These members of the Los Zetas organization were arrested by federal agents in 2007, along with their leader, the feared Eleazar Medina Rojas (not pictured).

The search for solutions

Given all the global violence caused by drugs, people are searching for solutions. As we have seen, some police forces are trying to crack down on major drug cartels. Many people also support teaching everyone, especially kids, about the dangers of drugs, in the hopes of stopping the demand for drugs in the future.

Some people argue that **decriminalizing** drugs will stop the violence. There are many arguments for and against this. (See the box below and the box on page 45 for both sides of this issue.)

ARGUMENTS FOR DECRIMINALIZING DRUGS

There are passionate arguments for and against decriminalizing drugs. The following are some of the major arguments in favor of decriminalization. See page 45 for the arguments against this. (Few people are arguing that hard drugs like heroin or cocaine should be legal, however. These discussions are mainly about marijuana.)

1. Decriminalizing drug possession and use would create jobs and raise billions of dollars in taxes. Legal marijuana farms would have to hire workers and pay taxes like any other farm business.

2. It would also cut deeply into drug cartels' profits. Marijuana is the number-one drug **exported** from Mexico. If marijuana were legal, people would buy it from legal sources, and the drug cartels would go bankrupt.

3. Gun violence would go down. Much of the drug violence in the United States is between warring factions of the drug cartels, or between cartels and police. Making drugs legal would eliminate this violence. It would also eliminate the need for the cartels to buy guns from the United States. Finally, cheaper, legal drugs would mean users would not resort to armed robbery or other gun violence to get drugs.

In 2001 the idea of decriminalizing drugs was put to the test in Portugal, which decriminalized the possession and use of all drugs. Drugs are still illegal in Portugal, but people arrested for drugs are not sent to prison. Instead they are encouraged to enter a **rehabilitation** program and kick their habits.

Positive results

At the time, politicians and citizens predicted that all kinds of terrible things would happen—for example, that Portugal would become a "drug tour" destination with planes filled with drug addicts. Some people predicted that drug-related violence would skyrocket, and that the murder rate would rise as the international drug cartels claimed their parts of the drug trade.

Ten years later, none of that has happened. In fact, drug use in Portugal has fallen, and drug-related violence is way down. Murders are down, domestic violence numbers are down, and gun and knife crimes are down. Of course, all this good news probably is not due exclusively to decriminalization, but it is clear that decriminalization has had an impact on the country.

■ Advocates of decriminalizing drugs point to the success countries such as Portugal have had with decriminalization policies.

Decriminalization and Amsterdam

Some people argue that the city of Amsterdam, in the Netherlands, shows some of the problems with decriminalizing drugs.

It is illegal to sell marijuana and hashish in the Netherlands, but the government allows coffeehouses to sell them if they follow some hard rules: no advertising, no sale of hard drugs or alcohol, no sales to persons under the age of 18, no causing public nuisances, and no sales of more than 5 grams per transaction.

■ Because of its coffeehouses, Amsterdam has become a worldwide drug tourism destination, despite the recent drug violence in the country.

A spike in crime

Until recently there was not much drug-related violence in Amsterdam, and the city's tolerant policies were used as an example of how well decriminalization could work. In the last few years, however, drug-related violence has been on the upswing.

There have been more than 25 drug-related murders in Amsterdam since 2005, mostly in the marijuana-growing industry. Small-time growers have been attacked and killed by gangs and organized crime groups that want a part of the profitable business of growing marijuana, which brings in more than $3.4 billion in foreign money each year. For protection, small growers arm themselves with weapons, booby-traps, and attack dogs. In one growing house, Dutch police found a pit of sharpened stakes underneath the front doormat.

Because of the violent crime, some coffeehouses have been shut down. But most Dutch people do not think the violence means that the laws should be changed. For now, the coffeehouses are open—and tourists keep coming.

ARGUMENTS AGAINST DECRIMINALIZING DRUGS

1. If drugs were legal, addiction would skyrocket. When the threat of arrest or prison time is removed, and if drugs are cheaper and easier to get, everyone would want to use them and more people would become addicted.

2. Drug cartels would not go out of business—instead, they would become more powerful. If drugs are legal, the cartels will produce more drugs and sell them for cheaper prices than the legal competition, creating a **black market**.

3. Drug violence would go up. More people who get addicted means more people who need drugs—and these people may commit violent crimes to get them.

HOW CAN VIOLENT CRIME BE STOPPED?

Violent crime is clearly a problem, touching people of all ages in many different parts of the world. But what, exactly, is the best way to tackle this problem? People have many different theories about the best solutions.

Removing weapons from the streets

The first thing law enforcement or governments try to do is get weapons out of the hands of criminals. The following are examples of this approach in action throughout the world:

- In the United States, Canada, and Australia, gun buy-back programs are often effective.
- In the United Kingdom, stop and search laws (see page 31) result in removing knives from people on the streets.
- In South Africa, law enforcement regularly destroys all the small arms it seizes, making sure millions of illegal weapons are not resold to military groups, gangs, or other violent criminals.
- After the Bosnian war in the 1990s, millions of weapons were left behind in Eastern Europe. Today, governments are hard at work destroying them. For instance, Croatia destroyed 25,000 small arms and light weapons in March 2008 alone, and since 2005 Bosnia and Herzegovina has destroyed more than 3,250 tonnes (3,600 tons) of ammunition.

An effective strategy?

Whether these programs work is up for debate. On one hand, destroying military-grade ammunition in Europe has had an impact on violent crime rates. But small buy-back programs usually do not make much difference in violent crime rates—especially in the United States, where, as we have seen, it is relatively easy for criminals to get guns. In the United Kingdom, although thousands of knives have been taken through stop and search laws, the knife crime rates have not been affected. Although laws might not have prevented or reduced all violent crime, would things have been worse without the laws?

■ A pile of rifles awaits destruction at a military base in the Ukraine in 2007. This was part of the Ukranian government's effort to destroy more than 400,000 guns in two years.

CASE STUDY

Scotland

Scotland has had success with its approach to stopping violent crime. Part of its approach involves weapons amnesty, meaning that people are allowed to turn in guns and knives to authorities, with no questions asked. But this is not the whole picture.

The city of Glasgow, Scotland, has sky-high rates of gun and knife violence. In response, Scottish police created a special unit that focused on combating gun and knife crime there. First, they figured out what kinds of social issues contributed to violent crime—such as poverty, unemployment, and neglect.

They fed this information into a computer system, which could then track these patterns in different areas of Glasgow. Once the police understood what—and where—the problems were, they then went into those areas to help find solutions. For instance, the software was able to pinpoint areas where gangs were most active and gang-related violence was high.

Using a combination of weapons amnesty, beefed-up patrols, and community outreach programs, Scotland has been able to get rid of some of its violence.

Stopping violence at its roots

While getting weapons off the streets is part of the solution, the programs that really work are those that stop the violence at its roots—with kids and communities. The hope is that by getting to young people before they are exposed to guns and gangs, officials can prevent these kids from becoming criminals in the first place.

Anti-crime campaigns

U.S. schoolchildren are taught about the dangers of guns through dozens of national, state, and local programs. The National Crime Prevention Council and its well-known mascot, McGruff the Crime Prevention Dog, have programs such as "Be Safe and Sound in School" and "Celebrate Safe Communities" that target schools and neighborhoods throughout the United States. Many local programs have also proven effective.

People who commit violent crimes tend to be from unstable or violent homes. So, many programs try to reach kids who come from these backgrounds. "The Peacebuilders" is a violence prevention program used in Australia and the United States that helps schools teach kids leadership and coping skills. Kids learn things like how to praise others, how to avoid bullying, how to respect each other, and how to help each other.

Stopping violent crime does not mean simply ending it in the home, or in schools, or in neighborhoods—getting rid of violence for good means getting rid of it everywhere.

Local solutions

The following are examples of successful local programs that try to keep kids occupied in positive pursuits, rather than violent crime:

- In Fort Myers, Florida, as part of the "Success Through Academic and Recreational Support" (STARS) program, a large recreational facility was built to provide activities and classes in sports, art, dance, music, and more for at-risk youths. As a result, juvenile crime rates by kids ages 11 to 14 reduced by almost one-third. Even more impressive is that among 11- and 12-year-old offenders, the rate of repeat criminal behavior dropped 64.3 percent.

- Police, human service agencies, and local citizens joined together in Norfolk, Virginia, to combat crime in 10 high-crime neighborhoods. The program focused on creating new youth athletic leagues and a youth forum for teens. This program led to a 29 percent drop in crime in the targeted neighborhoods and a citywide reduction in violent crime.
- Several U.S. cities have begun a popular program of night basketball. In most places where night basketball leagues play, crime has gone down. For example, the original league in Glenarden, Maryland, is credited with reducing crime by 60 percent. In the Winton Hills section of Cincinnati, Ohio, crime rates plummeted 24 percent within 13 weeks after a late-night recreation program was created.

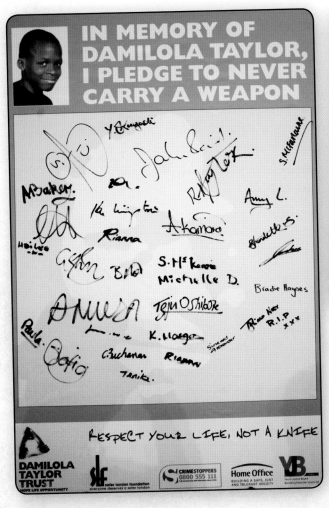

IN MEMORY OF DAMILOLA TAYLOR, I PLEDGE TO NEVER CARRY A WEAPON

RESPECT YOUR LIFE, NOT A KNIFE

DAMILOLA TAYLOR TRUST

CRIMESTOPPERS 0800 555 111

Home Office

THINK ABOUT IT

Especially in the United States, the idea of getting tough on crime through heavy prison sentences is a popular way to get violent criminals off the street. But tough prison sentences do not seem to work. Why do you think this is?

■ Damilola Taylor was only 10 years old when he was stabbed and killed on his way home from a library in London. The boys who attacked him were not much older than he was.

VIOLENT CRIME AND THE MEDIA: IS THE WORLD REALLY THAT SCARY?

The world can seem like a very violent place today.

To begin with, major forms of entertainment media are full of violence. Popular crime shows on television unravel stories of grisly murders or violent gang shootouts. Some of today's most popular movies feature action heroes in elaborate shootouts or scenes full of explosions and terror. Perhaps the most violent medium of all is video games. In games like *Grand Theft Auto*, players are rewarded for killing other people.

VIDEO GAMES AND VIOLENCE

Some people think that exposure to violence makes people numb to violent crimes. There is another argument, however, that expressing violent emotions through violent games gives people an outlet, which means they will not commit crimes in real life. What do you think? Do video games and movies make people, especially kids, more likely to commit violent acts?

■ Explosive headlines about violent crimes tend to be popular choices for the front page.

Violence in the news

Violence in entertainment is one thing, but news media can make you feel afraid that the real world is very violent as well. When you read newspapers and news websites or watch news on television, you can get the impression that the world is overrun with violent crime, and that no one is safe. But is it really true—is the world such a dangerous place?

Luckily, the answer is no—things are not really as bad as the media can make them seem. Generally, crime around the world is on the decline. Most local communities do not deal with a lot of violent crime. In fact, 37 percent of all violent crimes committed in the United States are in major cities, which make up only 20 percent of the country's total population.

Yet the media give a very different impression. Sensational murders, kidnappings, gang violence, and other violent crimes tend to be reported more than other news. This is because fear and danger are a lot more interesting to hear about than normal, everyday news. Major media outlets know that they will have more readers or viewers if their stories grab people's attention.

Be part of the solution

So, where does this leave you? On the one hand, it is important to be aware of the threats of violent crime and to make smart decisions in your daily life, such as not getting involved with gangs or drugs. These are common-sense decisions that everyone can make.

But the reality is that the world is not as violent as the media would lead you to believe, and that you should not live your life in fear. What you can do, however, is be part of the solution. Educate yourself about the dangers of violent crime and help others in your community to stay on the right path. If you make these changes now, you can give your community a safer future.

GLOSSARY

amendment change in something, such as a law or constitution

ammunition projectiles such as bullets that are fired from guns

black market refers to the illegal trade of goods

carjacking action of stealing a vehicle that has people in it

cartel group or organization that controls and limits production and
distribution

cell small, usually anonymous, group working for a larger organization

decriminalization to change the laws so that something is no longer a
crime

distribution network groups that work together to distribute drugs

export send a product to another country to be sold

grenade small, handheld bomb

homicide when one person kills another person

magazine part of a gun that holds bullets or other projectiles to be fired

narcotic drug used for nonmedical purposes, usually refering to an
illegal substance

per capita per person

pump action mechanism on a gun that allows the ammunition to be
quickly ejected and replaced

rehabilitation process of restoring someone to a healthy, normal life after
a problem such as drug addiction

semi-automatic firearm designed to fire a single cartridge, eject the
empty case, and reload the chamber each time the trigger is pulled

smuggle import or export goods illegally

stop and search police power in the UK that allows officers to search people without suspicion of a crime

surveillance monitoring a person or group

urban relating to a city or town

vigilante person who takes the law into his or her own hands

zero tolerance rule or rules that impose automatic punishment

FURTHER INFORMATION

There are many places where you can find out more about violent gun, knife, and gang crimes.

Books

Cefrey, Holly. *Gun Violence*. New York, NY: Rosen Publishing Group, 2008.

Lankford, Ronald. *Gun Violence*. Farmington Hills, MI: Greenhaven Press, 2006.

Pogrebin, Mark. *Guns, Violence, and Criminal Behavior*. Boulder, CO: Lynne Reinner Publishers, 2009.

Springwood, Charles. *Understanding Global Gun Cultures*. Oxford: Berg, 2007.

Websites

Dozens of websites give accurate, up-to-date information about violent crimes around the world. The most reliable sites are those maintained by government organizations, such as the United Nations, The World Health Organization, and NATO. World news organizations also post breaking stories about violence and violent crimes around the globe. Here is a list of resources to explore online:

United Nations Office on Drugs and Crime
http://www.unodc.org/

U.S. Drug Enforcement Administration
http://www.justice.gov/dea

UK Home Office online knife crimes resource
www.knifecrimes.org

Drug-related crime factsheet
http://www.whitehousedrugpolicy.gov/publications/factsht/crime/index.html

National Institute of Justice
www.ojp.usdoj.gov/nij

Bureau of Justice Statistics
http://bjs.ojp.usdoj.gov/

An article on gun control
www.enotes.com/public-health-encyclopedia/gun-control

A look inside gun shows
www.ucdmc.ucdavis.edu/vprp/

An article on youth, gangs, and guns
www.centerforinvestigativereporting.org/articles/youthsgangsandguns

United Nations document exploring firearm ownership around the world
http://www.unodc.org/documents/data-and-analysis/tocta/6.Firearms.pdf

An article on preventing crime
http://www.ncjrs.gov/pdffiles/171676.pdf

Topics for further research

There's nowhere on Earth where violent crime doesn't happen. But violent crime isn't always committed with guns and knives. These topics cover gun-related violent crime as well as other types of violent crimes that affect young people and adults every day, everywhere:

armed robbery
assault
bullying
domestic violence
drug smuggling
rape and sexual violence
weapons smuggling

INDEX